# my family and me

## and

### a family history fill-in book

HARPER

*An Imprint of* HarperCollins*Publishers*

ISBN 978-0-06-291484-2

Production by Stonesong
Interior Design and Typography by Jessica Nordskog
Interior Illustrations by Gina Luoma and Dan Nordskog
19 20 21 22 23   PC/LSCC   10 9 8 7 6 5 4 3 2 1

First Edition

This book belongs to:

..................................................................

With help from:

..................................................................

# Your Story

Every book ever written started with an idea. When you read a book, you are reading about what other people think and know.

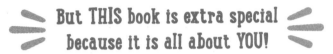

**But THIS book is extra special because it is all about YOU!**

Your family history is the story of you: who you are now, where you came from, how you got here, and all the people who helped to make today possible for you.

Genealogy is the study of your family's history. Genealogists are like detectives or reporters. They ask questions and follow clues.

When you study genealogy, you learn about all the people you're related to as far back in history as you can. You can find out where your ancestors came from and how they lived.

As you complete this book, you'll enlist the help of one of your relatives to do your own genealogy research. When you're done, you'll have a record of your family history that you can share with other members of your family. One day, you may even pass it down to your children and your grandchildren.

## THE INTERVIEWS

Interviewing people is how a lot of genealogists do research. Writing down what your relatives remember helps you get to know them. It helps you keep track of what their lives were like growing up. Once you write down a person's memories, you can share them with relatives who come after you—younger siblings, cousins, nieces, and nephews. Passing down stories that way is how history gets recorded. But first, someone has to write it down. **And now that *someone* is you!**

# How to use this book

This book was created for **you and an adult** in your family to work on together. It has activities and information just for you to fill out on your own. It has **quizzes** and **games** for you to fill out together. You'll also get a chance to interview your family member.

As you go through the activities, you'll learn a lot about who you are and where you come from. You'll get a much clearer picture of yourself, your family, and where you fit in.

Have fun filling out the pages. **Get creative and get colorful**—this is your book and your story after all!

Pages marked with one pencil can be filled out on your own.

Pages marked with two pencils are interview pages that you can fill out with your family member.

Pages marked with two people are activities you can do together.

Pages marked with a game board are activities you can do alone.

# My Family ♥

## What is a family?

All families are different, and all families are unique. No one's family is quite like yours. Some families have a mom and a dad, some have one parent, and others have two moms or two dads. Some kids have parents who got divorced and married other people, so they have stepparents and maybe even stepsiblings or half siblings. Some families have adopted children or foster children or no children at all. Some kids live with a family of aunts, uncles, grandparents, sisters, brothers, cousins, foster parents, adoptive parents, or guardians who take care of them.

*There's no end to the different ways a family can look.* ♥

## What do all types of families have in common?

# LOVE

Color and decorate the letters!

# Relative Terms

A relative is a person who is part of your family. They can be related by blood, marriage, adoption, or just by love. Test your knowledge of relative terms below!

A man who marries your mother ········► **restpatfeh** _____

Your mother's mother ········► **romdarngeth** _____

A brother you share only
one parent with ········► **floh breathr** _____

Your father's sister ········► **tuna** _____

Your mother's brother's child ········► **ucoins** _____

Your father's grandfather ········► **garde threagnraft** _____

Your mother's sister's husband ········► **ecnul** _____

*See page 122 for the answers!*

## Dozens of cousins

If you come from a big family, you probably have a lot of cousins. You may have a lot of second and third cousins, too, but do you know what that means?

**First cousin:** people who share **grandparents.**

**Second cousin:** people who share **great-grandparents.**

**Third cousin:** people who share **great-great-grandparents.**

When you get to cousins of your parents and grandparents, they are named by how far removed they are from you. Your dad's first cousin is your first cousin once removed; her son is your second cousin. Your grandmother's first cousin is your first cousin twice removed.

# ALL ABOUT ME

This is what I look like today.

Draw your picture or place a photo here.

Your name here!

**My name is** _____

My birthday is _____

I was born in _____

I am _____ years and _____ months and _____ days old today

I like to play _____
_____

I live in _____

I've lived in _____ places so far

My favorite hobbies are _____
_____

My favorite thing to study or read about is _____

Today's date _____

# ALL ABOUT YOU

Now ask your relative to fill out the information on this page.

This is what I look like today.

Draw your picture or place a photo here.

Your name here!

**My name is** _____

My birthday is _____

I was born in _____

I am _____ years and _____ months and _____ days old today

I like to play _____

_____

I live in _____

I've lived in _____ places so far

My favorite hobbies are _____

_____

My favorite thing to study or read about is _____

Today's date _____

# Me as a baby

## What I was like as a baby:

My favorite thing when I was a baby was _____

My first word was _____

Fill in the space below with a story about yourself when you were little. Can't remember anything? Ask your family member for suggestions.

### When I was a baby, I . . .

_____

_____

_____

_____

_____

_____

_____

_____

# When we first met...

Tell me about the day we first saw each other.

How old was I?

How old were you?

What can you remember about that day?

# Family Tree

Families come in all sizes. No two families are alike. What does your family tree look like? Write your name in the center on the trunk. Then create branches or leaves for all of the people in your life who make up your family.

## What makes a family?

All families are different, and all families are special. Your family can be made up of a mix of many people, including parents, stepparents, foster parents, grandparents, brothers and sisters, half siblings, step-siblings, aunts, uncles, cousins, and friends. Just because you're not related to people by blood doesn't mean they aren't family!

Friends are the
family we choose
for ourselves.

# Family Crossword

## What makes a family?

See page 122 for the answers!

**ACROSS**

**3** a place where you and your family live

**4** to divide something evenly

**6** a boy who has the same parents as you

**7** how you feel when you spend time with family

**DOWN**

**1** what you feel when you care about someone

**2** an animal that lives with you

**4** a girl who has the same parents as you

**5** a very young child

**7** wrap your arms around someone in a loving way

# FAMILY WORD CLOUD

A word cloud is a picture made up of words that are related to each other. The size of each word shows how important it is compared to the other words.

## Here's a word cloud about pets.

furry

fluffy meow **PET** bark

funny buddy love huggable

favorite

Create your own word cloud around the word FAMILY in the space below. We've started you off with a few of the basics. Fill in the rest of the words around it in the shape of a cloud. The words could be names of people in your family, things you like to do together, or how family makes you feel. Make more important words bigger. Get creative with the design and colors!

# INTERVIEW TIPS

You can learn a lot about someone just by asking questions. Even someone you think you know very well.

> **The person you are interviewing is called your SUBJECT.**
>
> **You are the INTERVIEWER or REPORTER.**

## Asking questions

Some of the questions in this book, like the ones that ask your interview subject's name, age, and where they live, are for recording basic facts. Other questions are made to trigger memories about things from a long time ago. And others are conversation starters to help you form a closer bond. In sharing your stories, you may realize how much you may have in common and how much you can learn from each other.

## Recording answers

If your subject speaks too quickly for you to write, you can record the conversation using a smartphone and transcribe it later, or you can ask the adult to write down their answers as you conduct the interview.

## PRO TIP

Small details tell big stories. If your subject gives you a one-word answer like "sometimes" or "yes," ask for more details. If your subject tells you a story and you want to know more, ask "what happened next?" or "how did you feel when that happened?"

# Every day

## Here are some of MY favorite things:

Food: _____

Place: _____

Subject in school: _____

Place I like to go with you: _____

Thing I own: _____

Day of the week: _____

Type of weather: _____

Thing to do on a rainy day: _____

## What are YOUR favorites?

_____

Food: _____

Place: _____

Subject in school: _____

Place you like to go with me: _____

Thing you own: _____

Day of the week: _____

Type of weather: _____

Thing to do on a rainy day: _____

# WHERE WE COME FROM

You can track the migration of your ancestors using a world map.

How far back can you trace your ancestors? List the names of all your relatives, as far back as you can go. Place a marker on the map for each person's birthplace and where they lived.

My birthplace:

_____

Your birthplace:

_____

Name of relative:

Birthplace:

# OUR FAVORITE MEMORIES

## Our best day together ever was

Where we were:

When was it?

What did we do?

Who else was there?

Draw a picture, make a list of things you did that day, or write about what happened that day.

# I remember...

Write a poem about your best day ever. Powerful poetry can come from things you remember. It can also come from the details you have forgotten. Fill in the blanks in the poem below to create your own memory poem.

I remember _____

I remember _____

I remember _____

I don't remember _____

But I'll always remember_____

The stick-together families are happier by far
Than the brothers and the sisters who take separate highways are.
The gladdest people living are the wholesome folks who make
A circle at the fireside that no power but death can break.

An exerpt from *The Stick-Together Families* by Edgar Guest

# THEN  AND NOW

| | Today | When you were my age |
|---|---|---|
| Most popular movie | | |
| Three biggest celebrities | | |
| Most popular song | | |
| President of the United States | | |
| What kids wear to school | | |
| Biggest news event | | |
| Most popular game or activity | | |
| Price of a candy bar | | |
| Cost of a movie ticket | | |

# THEN  AND NOW

Where did you live when you were my age?

_____

Who did you live with?

_____

When you were my age, what was a typical day like?

_____

_____

What did you do on the weekends with your friends?

_____

_____

What important world events were happening when you
were a kid? How did they affect you?

_____

_____

What was your favorite movie when you were my age?

_____

What did you want to be when you grew up?

_____

Where did you want to live?

_____

# Before we were a family

What was your life like before me?

_____

Who did you live with?

_____

What city did you live in?

_____

Tell me about where you lived.
What did it look like?

_____

_____

_____

What did you like about it?

_____

_____

What did you do every day?
Did you go to work or school?

_____

_____

_____

# FAN-TASTIC

| FAVORITE |  Me |  You |
|---|---|---|
| Superhero | | |
| Cartoon | | |
| Book | | |
| Band or artist | | |
| Famous person | | |
| Candy | | |
| Restaurant | | |

If you could go out for treats with one person, living or dead, across all of history, who would it be and why?

Who would it be?_____

Why?_____

Where would you go?_____

What would you order?_____

What would they order?_____

# Quiz time

How are you alike? How are you different?
Take this quiz to get your compatibility score.

Sweet or salty

Snow or rain

Loud or quiet

Crowded or empty

Fancy or casual

Sports car or limousine

Soda or water

Winter or summer

Stay home or go out

**Count up** the number of times your answers matched.

**Check** your numbers to see how alike or different you are.

## 14-20:

You're like two peas in a pod! You never have trouble deciding what to do because you're always in sync.

Early morning or late night

Books or movies

Camping out or stylish hotel

Cats or dogs

Chocolate or vanilla

Water park or amusement park

Chocolate chip or oatmeal cookie

Animated or live action

Slide or swings

School or summer camp

Dance or sing

Video games or board games

## 7-13:
You're a lot alike! You share many of the same interests but also like to do things on your own. You'll always be able to find common ground.

## 0-6:
You're as different as different can be, but that's what makes a family! You'll never run out of new things to introduce to each other and you should never stop trying!

# Two truths and a lie

How well do you know each other? For this activity, each of you writes down two things that are true and one that isn't true, in any order. Look at the other person's list and see if you can guess which is the lie!

**ME:**

1. _____

2. _____

3. _____

Your guess:

- - - - - - - - - - - - - - - - - - - - - - - - - - - - - - -

**YOU:**

1. _____

2. _____

3. _____

My guess:

- - - - - - - - - - - - - - - - - - - - - - - - - - - - - - -

# INTERVIEW TIME

Pull up a chair. Grab a cup of tea. Sharpen your pencils.
It's time for a little Q & A. Ask your family member these
questions and write their answers here.

Who's the oldest relative you remember? What do you
remember about them? Are they still around?

_____

_____

How did your family celebrate holidays when you
were a child?

_____

_____

What was your first job?

_____

What did you do with your first paycheck?

_____

_____

What was your favorite job and why?

_____

_____

Who are some of your heroes?

_____

_____

# SNACK TIME

*Let's talk about food*

| FAVORITE | Me | You |
|---|---|---|
| Breakfast | | |
| Lunch | | |
| Dinner | | |
| Vegetable | | |
| Fruit | | |
| Type of cookie | | |
| Recipe to make | | |
| Holiday food | | |
| Milkshake flavor | | |

Which of our relatives is the best cook? _____

Who is the worst cook? _____

What one food would you eat every day
for the rest of your life if you could? _____

What's the weirdest thing that you like to eat that
other people probably think is totally gross? _____

# REEL FUN
## Let's talk about movies

| FAVORITE | Me | You |
|---|---|---|
| Movie genre or style | | |
| Comedy | | |
| Nonfiction movie | | |
| Animated film | | |
| Live action | | |
| Scary movie | | |
| Movie that always makes me cry | | |
| Movie that always makes me think | | |

If my life were a movie,
its title would be _____

_____ would play me.
name of celebrity

_____ would play you.
name of celebrity

# What's in a name

**What does my name mean?**

**Where did my name come from?**

**If I could change my name, it would be:**

**What does your name mean?**

**Where did your name come from?**

**If you could change your name, what would you change it to?**

I usually call you

You usually call me

These are my nicknames:

These are your nicknames:

## Write a story together.

- The person whose birthday is closest gets to go first.
- Write only six words at a time, then give the pen or pencil to the other person.
- When they have written exactly six words, even if they are in the middle of a sentence or thought, it's your turn again.
- Can you write a whole story together six words at a time?
- Give the story a title when you're done.

title

# THE FAMILY CATEGORIES GAME

It's family game time! Using the letters in the word FAMILY, fill in the grid with words that start with the letters in the rows and fit into the categories. Fill out your answers separately and compare notes when you're done. How many of your answers matched?

| | Member of our family | A place we like to go | Something we love | Something we do together |
|---|---|---|---|---|
| **F** | | | | |
| **A** | | | | |
| **M** | | | | |
| **I** | | | | |
| **L** | | | | |
| **Y** | | | | |

## Need an example?

For the category "Member of our family" in the A column, you could say "Aunt," "Alice," "accountant" or any other A-word that is either a name or description of someone in your family.

| | Member of our family | A place we like to go | Something we love | Something we do together |
|---|---|---|---|---|
| **F** | | | | |
| **A** | | | | |
| **M** | | | | |
| **I** | | | | |
| **L** | | | | |
| **Y** | | | | |

# Our friends

### Best friend

Me        You

### First friend

Me        You

### Funniest friend

Me        You

### Easiest person to talk to

Me        You

### Best person to go on an adventure with

Me        You

### Best person to sit around doing nothing with

Me        You

### Most interesting friend

Me        You

### Best person to do a project with

Me        You

### Friend who gets along with everyone

Me        You

### Friend you would do anything for

Me        You

# INTERVIEW TIME

## Ask your family member these questions and write their answers here.

Who was your best friend growing up?

_____

How did you meet each other?

_____

What kinds of things did you do with your friends when you were my age?

_____

_____

Tell me a story about a funny adventure you had with a friend as a kid.

_____

_____

_____

_____

_____

_____

# BINGO

**Place an X on all of the things you can do.**

Me

| B | I | N | G | O |
|---|---|---|---|---|
| Touch your nose with your tongue | Walk on your hands | Recite the alphabet backward | Read someone's lips | Solve a Rubik's Cube |
| Sew a button onto a shirt | Ride a bicycle | Do a back bend | Stand on your head | Make a paper airplane |
| Hop on one foot 30 times | Fold origami | Count to ten in another language | Cook dinner | Throw a football spiral |
| Blow a bubble gum bubble | Sign a word in sign language | Curl your tongue | Blow up a balloon | Juggle two or more objects |
| Tread water for 60 seconds | Use chopsticks | Whistle | Raise one eyebrow | Play a musical instrument |

## You

| B | I | N | G | O |
|---|---|---|---|---|
| Touch your nose with your tongue | Walk on your hands | Recite the alphabet backward | Read someone's lips | Solve a Rubik's Cube |
| Sew a button onto a shirt | Ride a bicycle | Do a back bend | Stand on your head | Make a paper airplane |
| Hop on one foot 30 times | Fold origami | Count to ten in another language | Cook dinner | Throw a football spiral |
| Blow a bubble gum bubble | Sign a word in sign language | Curl your tongue | Blow up a balloon | Juggle two or more objects |
| Tread water for 60 seconds | Use chopsticks | Whistle | Raise one eyebrow | Play a musical instrument |

Which one of you has filled up more spaces? Try doing a few of these together. See if you can teach each other new skills and fill in more boxes!

# ☯ Never have I ever

Are you ready to get to know each other a little better?
Write your initials next to anything you've done.
Leave anything you haven't done blank.

Eaten raw cookie dough _____

Gotten caught picking my nose _____

Comforted someone when they were sad _____

Cut my own hair _____

Lied to a teacher _____

Worn clothes inside out all day
without noticing _____

Eaten something off the floor _____

Broken a bone _____

Had ice cream for breakfast _____

Stayed up all night _____

Pretended I liked something when I didn't _____

Fallen asleep in class _____

Sung karaoke _____

Gotten gum stuck in my hair _____

Gotten into a fight with a friend _____

Had a cavity _____

Been bullied _____

Gotten spooked at a haunted house _____

Gotten a strike in bowling _____

Been out of the country _____

Eaten expired food _____

Cried while watching a sad movie _____

Lied about my age _____

# Getting to know you

## A board game for 2 players ● Need: 1 coin, 2 game pieces

Flip the coin to start. The first person to get heads goes first. On your turn, flip the coin. If it comes up heads, move your piece two spaces. If you get tails, move one space. Read what's on the space out loud and give your answer. Continue taking turns until you both reach the finish!

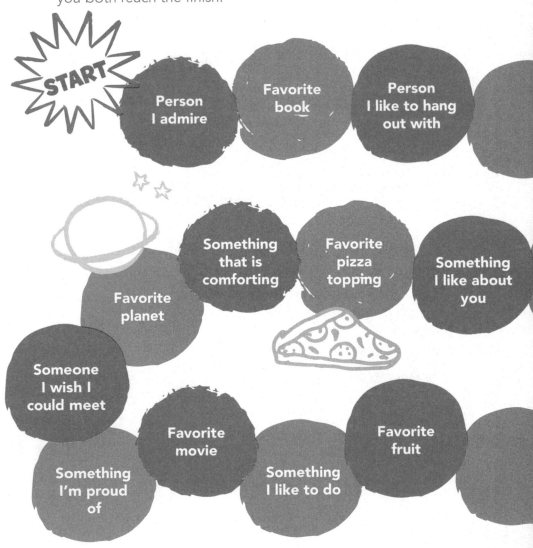

START

Person I admire

Favorite book

Person I like to hang out with

Something that is comforting

Favorite pizza topping

Something I like about you

Favorite planet

Someone I wish I could meet

Favorite movie

Favorite fruit

Something I'm proud of

Something I like to do

Favorite candy

Something that makes me smile

Invent a flavor of ice cream

Place I'd like to visit

Favorite animal

Something I'm excited for

Favorite sport

Favorite activity

Happiest day of the week

Happiest time of day

Something I'm good at

Places I'd like to live

Favorite TV show

Invent a new sport

FINISH

43

# Things that are important to me

Three things I know are true:

_____

_____

_____

Today I feel like telling you . . .

_____

_____

Some of the best advice I have ever received is . . .

_____

_____

The best advice I would give you is . . .

_____

_____

_____

# Their turn

**Ask your family member these questions and write their answers here.**

What do you feel like telling me about today?

_____

_____

_____

What is the best advice you have ever received?

_____

_____

What advice do you have for me?

_____

_____

_____

_____

_____

# Happiness is...

What makes me happy:

What makes me sad:

What cheers me up:

What makes you happy?

What makes you sad?

What cheers you up?

# Draw something that makes you happy here:

How are you alike? How are you different?
Take this quiz together and find out.

Read the questions below and place your
initials next to your choices for each one.

## Would you rather . . .

_____ Read a book **or** watch a movie? _____

_____ Have a monkey as a pet **or** live with monkeys in the wild? _____

_____ Draw a picture **or** tell a story? _____

_____ Time travel to the past **or** the future? _____

_____ Be a wizard **or** a superhero? _____

_____ Be thought of as wise **or** funny? _____

_____ Be a kid **or** be an adult? _____

_____ Have the power to be invisible **or** the power to read minds? _____

Spend a day playing _____ at the beach **or** in the snow? _____

Eat vegetable-flavored _____ ice cream **or** ice-cream-flavored vegetables? _____

Ride the biggest roller _____ coaster in the world **or** float on a mile-long lazy river? _____

_____ Live in a space station **or** in an underwater city? _____

# Weird and Wacky
# INTERVIEW QUESTIONS

Ask your family member these questions to get to know them better. Then turn the tables and let your family member ask you the same questions.

What game, movie, or TV show would you like to live in for a day?

What song have you completely memorized?

Are you usually early, on time, or late for things?

What is one thing you would change about yourself if you could?

Where's a place you've been that you never want to go back to?

Where would you live if you could move anywhere in the world?

What would you do if you had a million dollars to spend any way you'd like?

What's the farthest you've ever traveled from home?

What's something that everyone else loves that you can't stand?

What's the best compliment you've ever received?

Who inspires you to be a better person and why?

Where do you feel completely out of place?

Where's one place you can go and always feel like you belong?

What did you argue about with your family when you were younger?

What is one question you've always wanted to know the answer to?

# I'm the expert!

## What is something you know a lot about?

On this page, have your family member ask you questions and write down your answers.

I know a lot about:

Here are some cool things I know:

Here's where I look when I want to find out more about it:

Your space: create a doodle, word cloud, or picture relating to the subject you are an expert on.

# You're the expert!

On this page, interview your family member and write down their answers.

**What is something you know a lot about?**

**Tell me five cool facts about it.**

1. _____
2. _____
3. _____
4. _____
5. _____

**How do you know so much about it?**

**What got you interested in it?**

# WINTER

**What I love about winter:**

**What do you love about winter?**

Draw a picture of your favorite winter activity or a place you'd like to go in winter.

# SPRING

What I love about spring:

What do you love about spring?

Draw a picture of your favorite spring flowers, foods, places, or activities.

# SUMMER

**What I love about summer:**

**What do you love about summer?**

Fill in the picture with your favorite things to do at the beach.

# FALL

**What I love about fall:**

**What do you love about fall?**

Fill in the scene with your favorite things about fall.

Your family history goes farther back than one generation. Some families can trace their ancestors back five or more generations while others can only get as far back as their grandparents. Together with the person you're completing this book with, interview your oldest living relatives to reach as far back into your family's past as you can. See if any of your family kept records that go back farther than anyone can remember. Write down what you learn here on this page.

**For each relative you interview, ask the following questions:**

**Relative's name:** _____

How are we related? _____

What were your parents' names? _____

Where did they live? _____

What did they do for a living? _____

How many siblings did they have? _____

What do you know about their grandparents? _____

**Relative's name:** _____

How are we related? _____

What were your parents' names? _____

Where did they live? _____

What did they do for a living? _____

How many siblings did they have? _____

What do you know about their grandparents? _____

**Relative's name:** _____

How are we related? _____

What were your parents' names? _____

Where did they live? _____

What did they do for a living? _____

How many siblings did they have? _____

What do you know about their grandparents? _____

**Relative's name:** _____

How are we related? _____

What were your parents' names? _____

Where did they live? _____

What did they do for a living? _____

How many siblings did they have? _____

What do you know about their grandparents? _____

**Relative's name:** _____

How are we related? _____

What were your parents' names? _____

Where did they live? _____

What did they do for a living? _____

How many siblings did they have? _____

What do you know about their grandparents? _____

# HOW EMBARRASSING!

This is my most embarrassing moment:

What is your most embarrassing moment?

# Future History

What do you think the world will be like in ten years?

### My turn

### Your turn

# PROUD MOMENTS

**These are my proudest moments:**

My greatest achievement so far

Something that comes easily to me (but may be hard for others) is

A time when my hard work paid off

The skill I'm most proud of

# PROUD MOMENTS

## What are your proudest moments?

What is the biggest challenge you faced as a kid? How did you overcome it?

What is your greatest achievement so far?

Can you think of a time when your hard work paid off?

What skill are you most proud of?

# Family History
## WORD SEARCH

| | | |
|---|---|---|
| ALIKE | ANCESTOR | ANSWER |
| ASK | BIRTH | BOOK |
| CURIOUS | DIFFERENT | FAMILY |
| GENEALOGY | GENERATION | HISTORY |
| INFORMATION | INTERVIEW | LEARN |
| NAME | PHOTOGRAPH | PUZZLE |
| QUESTIONS | RECORDS | RESEARCH |
| SEARCH | SURPRISE | TOGETHER |

*See page 122 for the answers!*

```
L L H A C T U S P P J T K I W
F N P F N X D K H M F Z C N E
Y X O R J R V O D X K S W F I
B G A N O I T A R E N E G O V
Y E O C G O B T K O A A S R R
L R E L G D O O I S N F U M E
E R O R A G R T O P S D R A T
Q K A T E E S E U K W S P T N
Z P I T S C N Z S F E U R I I
H W H L U I Z E H E R O I O H
O E G Q A L H Y G X A I S N T
R O T S E C N A M E S R E M R
D I F F E R E N T I K U C H I
M L W R J U C Q X B P C K H B
H C R A E S E T F A M I L Y F
```

# ON THE JOB

**Ask your family member these questions and write their answers here.**

What do you do or did you do for work?

_____

What is the hardest part about what you do every day?

_____

What is the hardest part about being a grown-up?

_____

Tell me one thing that happened to you that changed your life.

_____

What is the greatest life lesson you've learned?

_____

How did you learn it?

_____

What is your dream for your future?

_____

What is your biggest success on the job or in your life?

_____

# My dream job

When I grow up, I want to be a _____.

I want to live in _____ with _____.
                    name of place

One thing that I hope will stay the same about me when I'm older

_____

One thing I'm looking forward to about being a grown-up

_____

Draw a picture of your dream for the future.

# Celebrations

My favorite holiday is

I love it because

What is your favorite holiday?

What makes it your favorite?

Have a birthday party _____ and invite 150 guests **or** invite just a few close friends?_____

_____ Fly on the back of a dragon **or** swim on the back of a dolphin?_____

_____ Have the power to fly **or** be able to teleport any place you want to go? _____

_____ Live in a fairy tale **or** a cartoon? _____

_____ Have lots of money **or** be famous? _____

Have a conversation _____ over the phone **or** over text message? _____

Be able to do anything you _____ want and not get in trouble **or** live in a world where everyone always does the right thing? _____

Never have homework _____ but learn only a little **or** have a normal amount of homework and be the smartest person you know?_____

_____ Have the fastest computor **or** the most high-tech car? _____

_____ Do karaoke **or** play air guitar? _____

_____ Spend the day indoors **or** outdoors? _____

# Count how many times you made the same choice. How well do you match up?

_____ /23

# of same answers

# Celebration
## Double Puzzle

**1** Unscramble each of the clue words.

**2** Take the letters that appear in circles and unscramble them for the final message.

HYBTIDRA

WNE RYAE

RPYTA

OODF

TSREESNP

SOITELMEN

PCAYNOM

RATDONITI

*See page 123 for the answers!*

# I MUSTACHE YOU A QUESTION

Ask your relative the questions on these pages and come up with your own question that you feel you *mustache* them! Are there any questions they feel they *mustache* you?

If you owned a store, what would you sell?

What's the first thing you like to do when you get to the beach?

What's your favorite word?

Do you like surprises?

What's one thing that bugs you more than anything?

If you were an animal, which animal would you be, and why?

If you were offered a seat on a rocket ship to visit the moon, would you go?

What's your favorite amusement park ride?

Would you ever go on a roller coaster that went upside down?

Write your own question here:

71

# WHAT MATTERS MOST

Interview your family member to find out more about their values.

What qualities make someone a good person?

_____

_____

_____

What do you love most about me?

_____

_____

_____

What do you wish I would do more often?

_____

_____

_____

What are three qualities you look for in a friend?

_____

_____

_____

What would cause you to lose respect for someone?

_____

_____

_____

Name one person you really respect. Why do you respect them?

_____

_____

_____

Name one person you would most like to be like. Why?

_____

_____

_____

What values do you believe all people should live by?

_____

_____

_____

How do you cheer up a friend when they're sad?

_____

_____

_____

Tell me about a time you were really proud of me.

_____

_____

_____

# Oh my stars!

Your zodiac sign is determined by the position of the stars when you were born. Some people believe that the zodiac sign you were born under can affect your basic personality, your preferences, and even your behavior. Ask your relative what they think!

Do you believe in astrology and horoscopes?_____

Are you superstitious?_____

What sign are you?_____

My sign is _____

Have you ever wished on a star?_____

What did you wish for?

_____

_____

Did you ever have a good-luck charm?_____

Do you consider yourself a lucky person?

_____

_____

What was one time you felt really lucky?

_____

_____

_____

_____

# What's your sign? Does your sign match your personality?

## AQUARIUS
January 20–February 18

Quiet
Quirky
Original

## PISCES
February 19–March 20

Compassionate
Artistic
Gentle

## ARIES
March 21–April 19

Confident
Enthusiastic
Determined

## TAURUS
April 20–May 20

Reliable
Patient
Loyal

## GEMINI
May 21–June 20

Curious
Adaptable
Affectionate

## CANCER
June 21–July 22

Loyal
Generous
Stubborn

## LEO
July 23–August 22

Brave
Warmhearted
Cheerful

## VIRGO
August 23–September 22

Sincere
Practical
Kind

## LIBRA
September 23–October 22

Fair
Even-tempered
Social

## SCORPIO
October 23–November 21

Daring
Passionate
Insightful

## SAGITTARIUS
November 22–December 21

Idealistic
Independent
Generous

## CAPRICORN
December 22–January 19

Genuine
Responsible
Ambitious

# Design your own star signs

Connect the stars to form a constellation that represents you.
Give it a name. Describe what it is and what it expresses.
What are three traits people born under your new constellation
have in common?

## ME

**Name of constellation**

YOU

Name of constellation

# Like it or not

**My turn!**

## 3 THINGS I LOVE
1. _____
2. _____
3. _____

## 3 THINGS I CAN'T STAND
1. _____
2. _____
3. _____

## 3 THINGS I'VE NEVER TRIED
1. _____
2. _____
3. _____

## MY BIGGEST FEAR: _____

My biggest pet peeve: I can't stand it when . . .

_____

_____

One thing I love that no one else likes is:

_____

_____

# Like it or not

## 3 THINGS YOU LOVE

1. _____
2. _____
3. _____

## 3 THINGS YOU CAN'T STAND

1. _____
2. _____
3. _____

## 3 THINGS YOU'VE NEVER TRIED

1. _____
2. _____
3. _____

## YOUR BIGGEST FEAR: _____

Your biggest pet peeve: I can't stand it when . . .

_____

_____

One thing I love that no one else likes is:

_____

_____

# THE BEST PET

If I could have any animal for a pet, it would be a

_____

because

_____

_____

I would name it ↘

_____

If YOU could have any animal for a pet, what would it be and why?

_____

_____

_____

_____

Have you ever had a pet? Yes/No

Type of animal: _____

Name: _____

Tell me a story about a time you had a pet or wanted one.

_____

_____

# FAMILY FUN

```
Z  X  P  G  Y  L  T  F  R  F  C  T  W  G  V
O  C  Y  A  A  L  R  A  G  V  Y  M  U  A  X
T  E  R  T  D  U  A  I  O  A  B  E  C  D  J
P  Y  Q  N  I  P  D  S  J  D  M  A  N  X  Q
A  C  Q  R  L  I  I  R  E  H  T  E  G  O  T
R  M  E  G  O  R  T  R  O  I  K  B  S  C  M
T  T  N  L  H  T  I  L  O  E  R  U  U  A  B
Y  I  I  J  E  F  O  N  E  S  P  O  R  T  S
S  N  U  S  J  D  N  W  I  A  L  K  M  Z  G
D  T  Y  O  I  C  R  E  C  N  A  D  P  E  O
Y  D  K  T  S  V  Z  A  F  M  E  C  C  R  M
M  E  F  S  L  O  U  Z  T  U  V  E  V  Q  U
S  S  J  T  N  K  P  F  S  E  N  N  N  T  I
```

| | | | |
|---|---|---|---|
| CELEBRATE | DANCE | FUN | GAMES |
| HOLIDAY | JOKES | MEMORIES | PARTY |
| SING | TALK | TOGETHER | TRADITION |
| TRIP | VACATION | VISIT | WEEKEND |

*See page 123 for the answers!*

# ALIKE AND DIFFERENT

Family members have a lot in common. They also have a lot of things that set them apart from each other. A Venn diagram is a way to organize and compare information. Fill out the Venn diagram below by yourself or together. Put things unique to you in your circle and things unique to your relative in their circle. Put things you have in common in the middle where they meet.

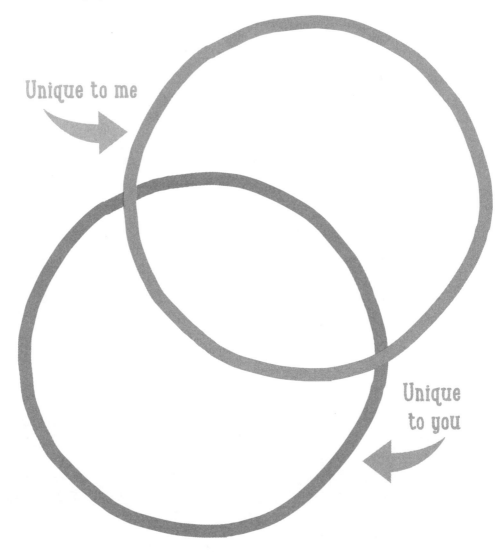

Unique to me

Unique to you

# SELFIE TIME!

Draw a picture of the two of you doing
something you love to do together.

# Traditions

**One thing that makes every family different is their traditions.**

My turn!

What is one thing that your family does differently than any other family you know?

_____

What are some of your favorite family traditions?

_____

_____

My least favorite family tradition is

_____

_____

My favorite holiday is _____

Here's a picture of how we celebrate it:

**Your turn!**

## Now ask your relative some questions.

How did my favorite family tradition get started?

_____

_____

_____

Did you have the same tradition growing up?

_____

_____

What was your favorite family tradition when you were my age?

_____

_____

What tradition do you wish we could carry on today from your childhood?

_____

_____

What was your least-favorite tradition from your childhood?

_____

_____

As we go along, our lives may change,
but family remains with us always.

# Invent your own NEW family holiday.

What would you call it?

## How would you celebrate it?

## We would eat

## We would play

## We would all wear

We would invite the following people

We would ask guests to bring

Our special holiday greeting would be

Here is a picture of our special new holiday

# WEEKENDS

Weekends are for

On the weekends, I like to

I wish I didn't have to

on the weekends.

I wish I could

every weekend.

# FREE TIME

**Ask your family member these questions and write their answers here.**

What do you like to do in your spare time?

_____

What did you like to do in your free time when you were a kid?

_____

How did you spend your weekends when you were my age?

_____

How do you spend your weekends now?

_____

What do you wish you had more free time to do?

_____

What do you wish you didn't have to do on the weekends?

_____

If you had a weekend with nowhere you had to be and nothing you had to do, how would you spend it? Who would you spend it with?

_____

_____

_____

# TELL ME A JOKE

**My favorite joke is:**

**What's your favorite joke or riddle from when you were my age?**

An inside joke is a joke based on something you experience together that only the people involved understand.

## Does your family have any inside jokes?
Share the story behind one of them here.

# Funny Stories

The funniest thing that ever happened to me was

I never get tired of the family story about the time when

But I'd be happy if I never heard the story about _____ again!

Tell me a funny story about your family when you were a kid.

# EVERY DAY

Everyone has a daily routine—things they do every day without even thinking about it. Our routines change over time. What is your routine like today, right now? How does it compare to your relative's daily routine?

| FAVORITE | Me | You |
|---|---|---|
| First thing you did when you woke up today | | |
| What did you eat for breakfast? | | |
| What did you have for lunch? | | |
| What's for dinner? | | |
| What are you wearing? | | |
| Name one thing you had to do today. | | |
| Who did you see? | | |
| Did you go anywhere? | | |
| What was one thing you really wanted to do today? Did you get to do it? | | |

What is your daily routine like?

Do you do the same thing every day, pretty much, or does it change depending on the day?

No matter what the day brings, you always

What is the last thing you do before you go to bed at night?

# My Bucket List

A bucket list is a list of things you want to do.

## MY LIST

1. _____
2. _____
3. _____
4. _____
5. _____
6. _____
7. _____
8. _____
9. _____
10. _____

**How many of these things can you do this week?**

_____

**This year?** _____

# Our Bucket List

Here is a list of things we want to do together.

## OUR LIST

1. _____
2. _____
3. _____
4. _____
5. _____
6. _____
7. _____
8. _____
9. _____
10. _____

**OUR PACT:**

**We promise to do at least one of these things by** _____
(date)

**Signed:** _____   _____
(me)                    (you)

# When I was a little kid . . .

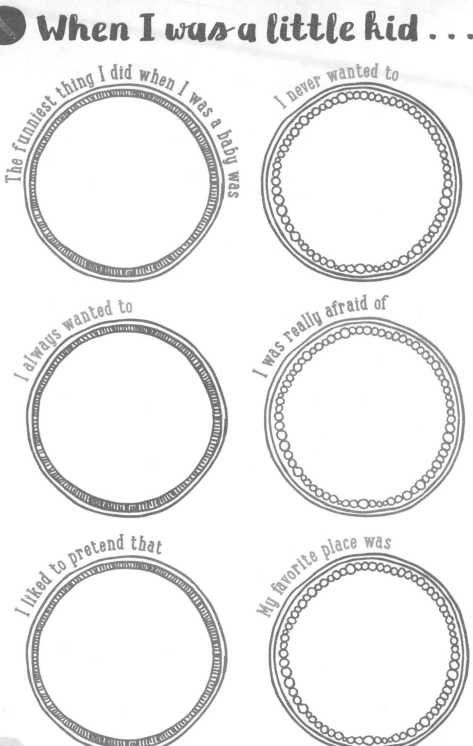

The funniest thing I did when I was a baby was

I never wanted to

I always wanted to

I was really afraid of

I liked to pretend that

My favorite place was

# When you were a kid . . .

What was your favorite color?

Did you have an imaginary friend?

What was your favorite game to play?

What is your earliest memory?

What was your favorite sport?

Who was your favorite athlete or sports team?

When you played pretend as a kid, what did you pretend?

Did you keep a journal or diary?

# WHAT I *love* ABOUT YOU

A family bond is a special thing. In many ways, our families know us better than anyone else. In the space below, write a list or make a word cloud of things you love about the person you're writing this book with.

Five words I would use to describe myself:

_____

_____

_____

_____

_____

Five words I would use to describe you:

_____

_____

_____

_____

_____

# WHAT DO YOU *love* ABOUT ME?

Make a list of things you love best about me!

_____     _____

_____     _____

_____     _____

_____     _____

What five words would you use to describe me?

_____     _____

_____     _____

_____

# Feelings

What being part of a family means to me:

_____

_____

_____

What does it mean to you to be part of a family?

_____

_____

_____

What do you feel when you think about home?

_____

_____

_____

What do you feel when you think about family?

_____

_____

_____

How should family members help each other?

_____

_____

_____

# EMOJIS

Every picture tells a story.
What emojis would you use to describe each other?

*Use this space to draw emojis for each other.*

# Questions

Are there questions you have for the person you are writing this book with that haven't been answered yet? Use this page to write your questions for your relative and their answers here.

1. _____

_____

2. _____

_____

3. _____

_____

4. _____

_____

5. _____

_____

6. _____

_____

7. _____

_____

8. _____

_____

# Questions

Ask your relative to ask you some questions.
Have them write their questions and your answers here.

1. _____
_____

2. _____
_____

3. _____
_____

4. _____
_____

5 _____
_____

6. _____
_____

7. _____
_____

8. _____
_____

# Hobbies

My favorite hobbies are

Your favorite hobbies are

Our favorite hobbies that we like to do together are

I would like to learn how to

What is something you would like to learn how to do?

# FAN FAVORITES

## I'm a big fan of _____

Here is why:

_____

_____

_____

_____

_____

_____

**#1**

## What are you fans of together?

Is there a TV show you never miss, a movie franchise you love, a sport you like to follow, an actor, musician, or athlete you know everything about together? Write about it here.

## We love _____

Here is why:

_____

_____

_____

_____

_____

_____

_____

_____

_____

_____

 # What if...

| FAVORITE | Me | You |
|---|---|---|
| If you could travel through time, when would you travel to? | | |
| If you were an inventor, what would you invent first? | | |
| If you could travel anywhere in the world, where would you go? | | |
| If you could travel through outer space, where would you go? | | |
| If you could have any job in the world, what would it be? | | |
| If you ruled the world, what is the first rule you would make? | | |
| If you could change one thing about yourself, what would it be? | | |

If you were going to spend two weeks on a deserted island, what would you take with you?

|  | Me | You |
| --- | --- | --- |
| 1. | | |
| 2. | | |
| 3. | | |
| 4. | | |
| 5. | | |
| 6. | | |
| 7. | | |
| 8. | | |
| 9. | | |
| 10. | | |

# SCHOOL DAYS

I am in _____ grade.

My teacher's name is _____.

There are _____ kids in my class.

To get to school in the morning, I _____.

Draw a picture of your school here.

**Ask your relative questions about when they were in the same grade you are now.**

What school did you go to? _____

How did you get to school? _____

How many kids were in your class? _____

Who was your teacher when you were my age? _____

Did you like your teacher? YES / NO
How come? _____

What did you have for lunch at school? _____

What did you like most about school? _____

What do you wish you could have changed about your school?

_____

_____

Did you have a lot of homework? _____

Did you get good grades? _____

Did you get along with your teachers? _____

Did you get along with your classmates? _____

# My award for you

**AWARD FOR**

BEST _____

Goes to _____

FOR _____

What I appreciate most about you

_____

_____ _____

_____ _____

_____ _____

# Your award for me

**AWARD FOR**

BEST _____

Goes to _____

FOR _____

What I appreciate most about you

_____

_____

_____

_____

# TAKEAWAYS

Things I learned from filling out this book together

_____

_____

_____

_____

_____

_____

_____

_____

_____

_____

_____

_____

_____

_____

_____

_____

The best thing about memories is making them.

_____

_____

_____

_____

The best thing about filling out this book together

_____

_____

_____

_____

_____

_____

_____

_____

_____

There's no
place like home.
-Dorothy

What surprised me most about filling out this book together

_____

_____

_____

_____

_____

_____

_____

_____

_____

_____

# The future

Ways I want to be like you when I'm older:

**1.**

**2.**

**3.**

**4.**

# The future

What do you wish for me?

**1.**

**2.**

**3.**

**4.**

# Genie in a Bottle

If you had three wishes for each other what would they be?

My wishes for you

1.

2.

3.

Your wishes for me

1.

2.

3.

# Yours Truly

Write a letter to the person you filled out this book with. Share how you feel about having this person in your family, what you learned about completing this book together, and maybe even write something you'd like to share that is hard to say out loud. When in doubt, you can list all the things you love or all the things you're grateful for!

## Parts of a letter

Always put the date on the top right of the page.

The greeting goes here.

March 17, 2019

Dear Grandma,

How are you? Things here are great! I just got back from a family vacation to the beach. We stayed right by the ocean! Every day we would swim and pick seashells.

The body of your letter is here. Indent new thoughts!

Are you happy that winter is over? I know that you don't like the cold temperatures. We're the same that way!

I will be visiting you soon. I can't wait to be at your house so we can bake together. I always have so much fun when I'm with you.

This is the closing.

Don't forget your signature!

Add doodles to brighten up the page.

Sincerely,

Pat

I ♥ you!

# Truly Yours

Now it's time for your relative to write a letter to you.
No peeking! Don't look over their shoulder while they're
writing—give them time and space to gather their thoughts
and compose their own special message!

## Silly sign-offs

Challenge your relative to come up with clever
acronyms for you to solve!

**YMF!**
You're My
Favorite!

**LYTM!**
Love You
the Most!

**SYS!**
Sending You
Smooches!

**F&FF!**
Family &
Friends
Forever

**LYFTS!**
Loved You from
the Start!

# Answers

**PAGE 7**

restpatfeh = **stepfather**

romdarngeth = **grandmother**

floh breathr = **half brother**

tuna = **aunt**

ucoins = **cousin**

garde threagnraft = **great-grandfather**

ecnul = **uncle**

**PAGE 14**

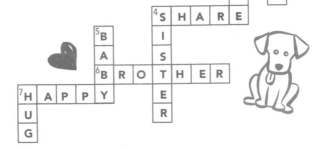

Crossword:
- ¹L ²P
- ³HOME / E T
- L V / T
- O
- ⁴SHARE
- ⁵B / I
- A / S
- ⁶BROTHER
- ⁷HAPPY / E
- U / R
- G

**PAGE 65**

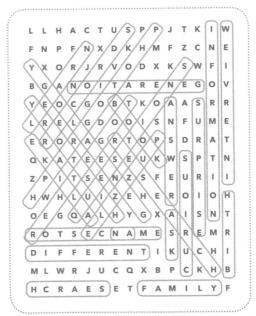

```
L L H A C T U S P P J T K I W
F N P F N X D K H M F Z C N E
Y X O R J R V O D X K S W F I
B G A N O I T A R E N E G O V
Y E O C G O B T K O A A S R R
L R E L G D O O I S N F U M E
E R O R A G R T O P S D R A T
Q K A T E E S E U K W S P T N
Z P I T S E N Z S F E U R I I
H W H L U I Z E H E R O I O H
O E G Q A L H Y G X A I S N T
R O T S E C N A M E S R E M R
D I F F E R E N T I K U C H I
M L W R J U C Q X B P C K H B
H C R A E S E T F A M I L Y F
```

## PAGE 69

birthday
new year
party
food
presents
milestone
company
tradition
Final answer: family time

## PAGE 81

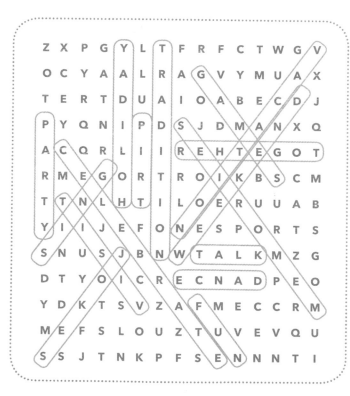

# IT'S ALL RELATIVE

## Step vs. Half vs. Full
What's the difference?

**Stepsiblings** are related through the marriage of one of their parents.

**Half siblings** are related by blood through one parent.

**Full siblings** are related by blood through both parents.

## Ancestor

A person who came before someone in a family tree, like a grandparent, a great-grandparent, or a great-great-grandparent or . . . well, you get the picture!

## Descendant

A person who comes after someone in a family tree, like a child, grandchild, great-grandchild, and so on.

## Genealogy

A study of the family, which seeks to identify ancestors and descendants, and find out more about them through research.

## Family history

The story of a family or families from ancestors to descendants. Genealogists conduct interviews and do research to discover the stories of a family's history. They write them down for future generations and other interested people.

## Foster parent

A person who officially takes a child into their family for a period of time without becoming the child's legal parent.

## Adoptive parent

Someone who goes through a legal process to become a child or children's permanent family.

## Guardian

Someone other than a parent who is legally responsible for taking care of a child's needs.

# KEEP ON LEARNING

If you've had fun learning about your past through connecting with your family member, keep the fun going with these activities, ideas, and resources.

**Ask your relatives** to go through old family photos with you and tell you stories about each of the pictures.

**Find a photo** of a relative from a long time ago who looks like you and try to re-create the photo with the same pose, hairstyle, and clothes.

**Go through old** family home movies. Many old images are on slides, film, or outdated video formats. Digitizing these archives makes a great gift for your family members!

**Create a timeline** of your family. Go as far back as you can, including important family dates like when people were born or got married, as well as important dates in history.

GRANDMA & GRANDPA
MARRIED

**Create your own** personal timeline from the day you were born to today. Add in digital photos. Start a new tradition to add more to your timeline from today on!

| BORN | START SCHOOL | TRIP TO FLORIDA | LEARNED TO RIDE A BIKE |

**Make a time capsule** of things that are important to you and your family today. Set a date five or ten or twenty years from now to open it.

**Start a tradition** to cook with your family member once a week or every holiday to learn your family recipes. Create a cookbook of all of the foods you make together.

**If you want to do more research on your family tree, check out some of these useful websites:**

www.USGenWeb.org

www.Ancestry.com

www.FamilySearch.org

# HOME
## is where the ♥ is!

Color in this page!